THE BOOK OF
2 Corinthians

ONE CHAPTER A DAY

GoodMorningGirls.org

The Book of 2 Corinthians

© 2020 Women Living Well Ministries, LLC

ALL RIGHTS RESERVED

No part of this book may be reproduced in any form or by any electronic or mechanical means, including information storage and retrieval systems, without written permission from the author, except in the case of a reviewer, who may quote brief passages embodied in critical articles or in a review.

Scripture is from the ESV® Bible (The Holy Bible, English Standard Version®), copyright © 2001 by Crossway Bibles, a publishing ministry of Good News Publishers. Used by permission. All rights reserved.

Welcome to Good Morning Girls! We are so glad you are joining us.

God created us to walk with Him, to know Him, and to be loved by Him. He is our living well, and when we drink from the water He continually provides, His living water will change the entire course of our lives.

> *Jesus said: "Whoever drinks of the water that I will give him will never be thirsty again. The water that I will give him will become in him a spring of water welling up to eternal life." ~ John 4:14 (ESV)*

So let's begin.

The method we use here at GMG is called the **SOAK** method.

> **S**—The S stands for *Scripture*—Read the chapter for the day. Then choose 1-2 verses and write them out word for word. (There is no right or wrong choice—just let the Holy Spirit guide you.)

> **O**—The O stands for *Observation*—Look at the verse or verses you wrote out. Write 1 or 2 observations. What stands out to you? What do you learn about the character of God from these verses? Is there a promise, command or teaching?

> **A**—The A stands for *Application*—Personalize the verses. What is God saying to you? How can you apply them to your life? Are there any changes you need to make or an action to take?

> **K**—The K stands for *Kneeling in Prayer*—Pause, kneel and pray. Confess any sin God has revealed to you today. Praise God for His word. Pray the passage over your own life or someone you love. Ask God to help you live out your applications.

SOAK God's word into your heart and squeeze every bit of nourishment you can out of each day's scripture reading. Soon you will find your life transformed by the renewing of your mind!

Walk with the King!

Courtney

WomenLivingWell.org, GoodMorningGirls.org

Join the GMG Community

Share your daily SOAK on **Facebook.com/GoodMorningGirlsWLW**

Instagram: WomenLivingWell #GoodMorningGirls

GMG Bible Coloring Chart

COLORS	KEYWORDS
PURPLE	God, Jesus, Holy Spirit, Saviour, Messiah
PINK	women of the Bible, family, marriage, parenting, friendship, relationships
RED	love, kindness, mercy, compassion, peace, grace
GREEN	faith, obedience, growth, fruit, salvation, fellowship, repentance
YELLOW	worship, prayer, praise, doctrine, angels, miracles, power of God, blessings
BLUE	wisdom, teaching, instruction, commands
ORANGE	prophecy, history, times, places, kings, genealogies, people, numbers, covenants, vows, visions, oaths, future
BROWN/GRAY	Satan, sin, death, hell, evil, idols, false teachers, hypocrisy, temptation

Introduction to the Book of 2 Corinthians

The book of 2 Corinthians is Paul's second letter to the Corinthians. In Paul's first letter, he reprimanded the church for their divisions, disorder, and lack of love inside the church. After they received the letter, Titus informed Paul that the church had repented of their sins but that there were some false teachers challenging Paul's authority in the church. So, Paul wrote a second letter to the church at Corinth.

This letter is different from the first letter because it's very personal. There are details in this book about Paul's personal life, that are found nowhere else in the New Testament. Paul is thankful for their repentance and obedience to the Lord and he writes to comfort them. Paul explains some of the hardships he has endured for the sake of Christ and also shares about a personal thorn in the flesh, that has kept him dependent on God. He then goes on to exhort the believers to live with a heart of forgiveness and generosity towards others. He calls them to live separate from the world and he ends the letter by warning them against false teachers.

The Purpose: Paul wrote a second time to the Corinthians to comfort, encourage and instruct them. He was overjoyed to hear that they were obeying the Lord and he encouraged them to press on in their obedience to the Lord through forgiveness and generosity. He also warned them to be on guard against false teachers.

The Author: Paul the Apostle.

Time Period: Around 55-57 A.D.

Key Verse: 2 Corinthians 5:17

> *Therefore, if anyone is in Christ, he is a new creation. The old has passed away; behold, the new has come.*

The Outline:

1. Introduction (1:1-2)
2. Paul's Ministry Explained (1:3-7:16)
3. Generosity Encouraged (8—9)
4. Defense Against False Teachers (10-12)
5. Conclusion (13)

The book of 2 Corinthians is an encouraging book. It is going to both comfort and challenge you. Some of the chapters are long, so be sure to leave at least 20 minutes for your reading each day. I can't wait to see how God reveals himself personally to each of us, as we read the book of 2 Corinthians together, chapter by chapter. So, let's get started!

Keep walking with the King!

Courtney

Blessed be the God of all comfort,

who comforts us in all our affliction,

so that we may be able to comfort

those who are in any affliction.

2 Corinthians 1:3&4

Reflection Question:

There was purpose in the afflictions of Paul. Paul experienced the comfort of God and as a result was able to comfort others, with the comfort he had received. The word comfort here means to lessen the sadness of someone and strengthen them with hope.

Not only is God our comforter in difficult times, but he wants to use us to be a comfort to others. There is purpose behind our pain, but we must first be humble enough to admit that we need the comfort of God, in order to receive it. Do you need God's comfort today? Ask him for it. Then name a time when you were hurting, and God comforted and strengthened you. How did God do that? And in what ways can you be a comfort to someone else?

2 Corinthians 1

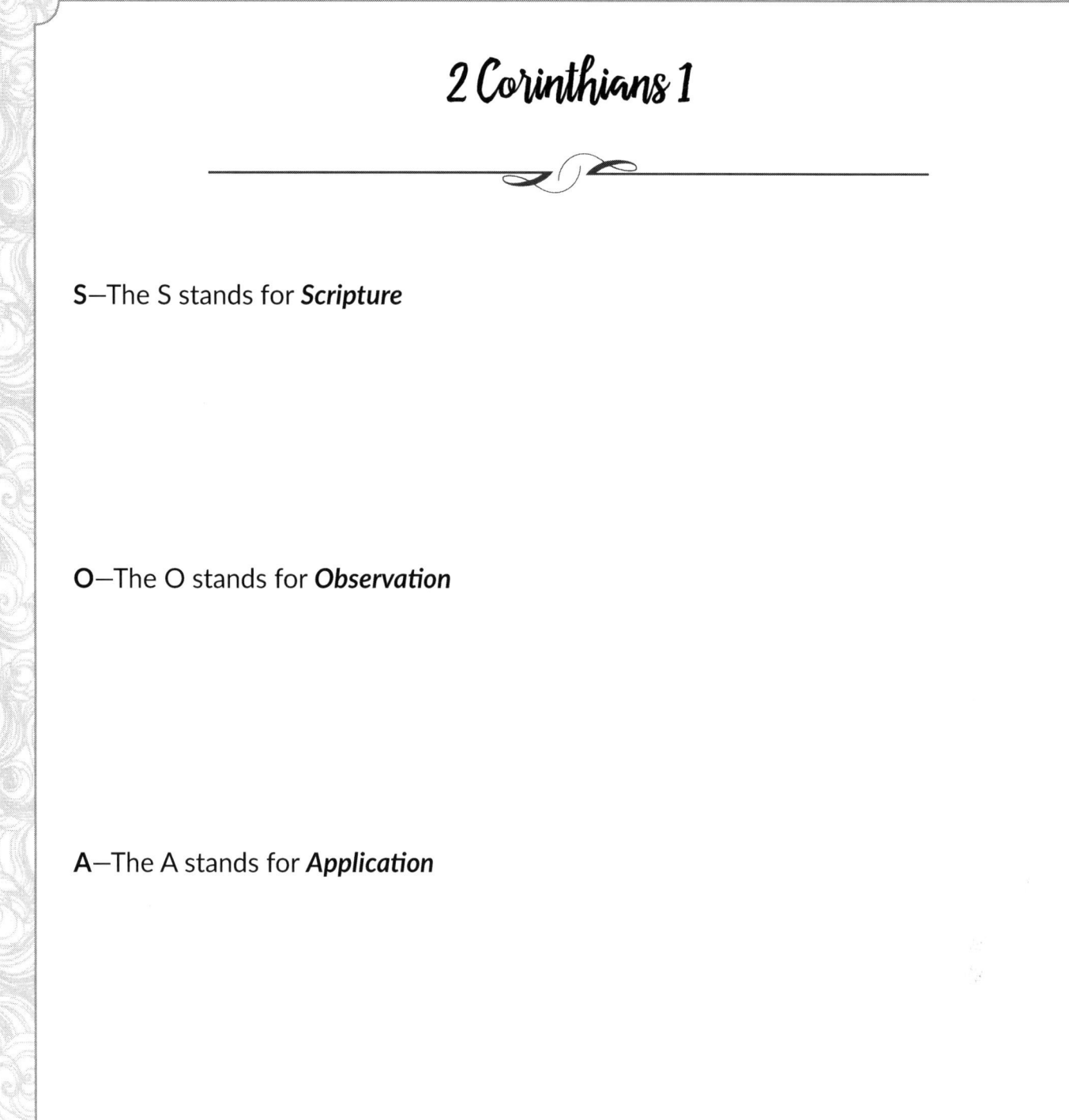

S—The S stands for *Scripture*

O—The O stands for *Observation*

A—The A stands for *Application*

K—The K stands for *Kneeling in Prayer*

I beg you to

reaffirm your love for him.

2 Corinthians 2:8

Reflection Question:

Paul emphasized the importance of the church forgiving and loving someone who had fallen into sin and then repented. In verse 10, he warns the church to be aware of the schemes of Satan. Satan likes to use a person's mistakes along with the condemnation of believers, to ruin a person who could be experiencing freedom, love, joy, peace, victory and fellowship.

Are you aware of the enemy's tactics? Do not be fooled. We become tools in the hands of Satan, when we will not extend love to someone who has sought forgiveness. Now that you are aware of this device that the enemy uses, can you think of someone who needs your love reaffirmed to them? How can you be used by God to show them love this week?

2 Corinthians 2

S—The S stands for *Scripture*

O—The O stands for *Observation*

A—The A stands for *Application*

K—The K stands for *Kneeling in Prayer*

Where the Spirit of the Lord is, there is freedom.

2 Corinthians 3:17

Reflection Question:

Within the trinity, there is God the Father, God the Son and God the Holy Spirit. They are three in one. Verse 17 tells us that the Lord is Spirit and where the Spirit of the Lord is, there is freedom. Because of Christ's death on the cross, we have direct access to God the Father and the Holy Spirit inside of us. We are never alone. He both guides and comforts us and has freed us from our sin and the law.

The freedom that comes from the Lord is not a freedom to disobey God. That is a twisted freedom rather than a spirit filled freedom. The freedom that comes from the Lord is a freedom from the need to strive or despair over our sin. We can rest in the Lord and live forgiven and free. Are you living free? Do you take advantage of the freedom the Spirit has given you? In what area are you not free and you need to be freed? Pray and ask the Lord to help you live free.

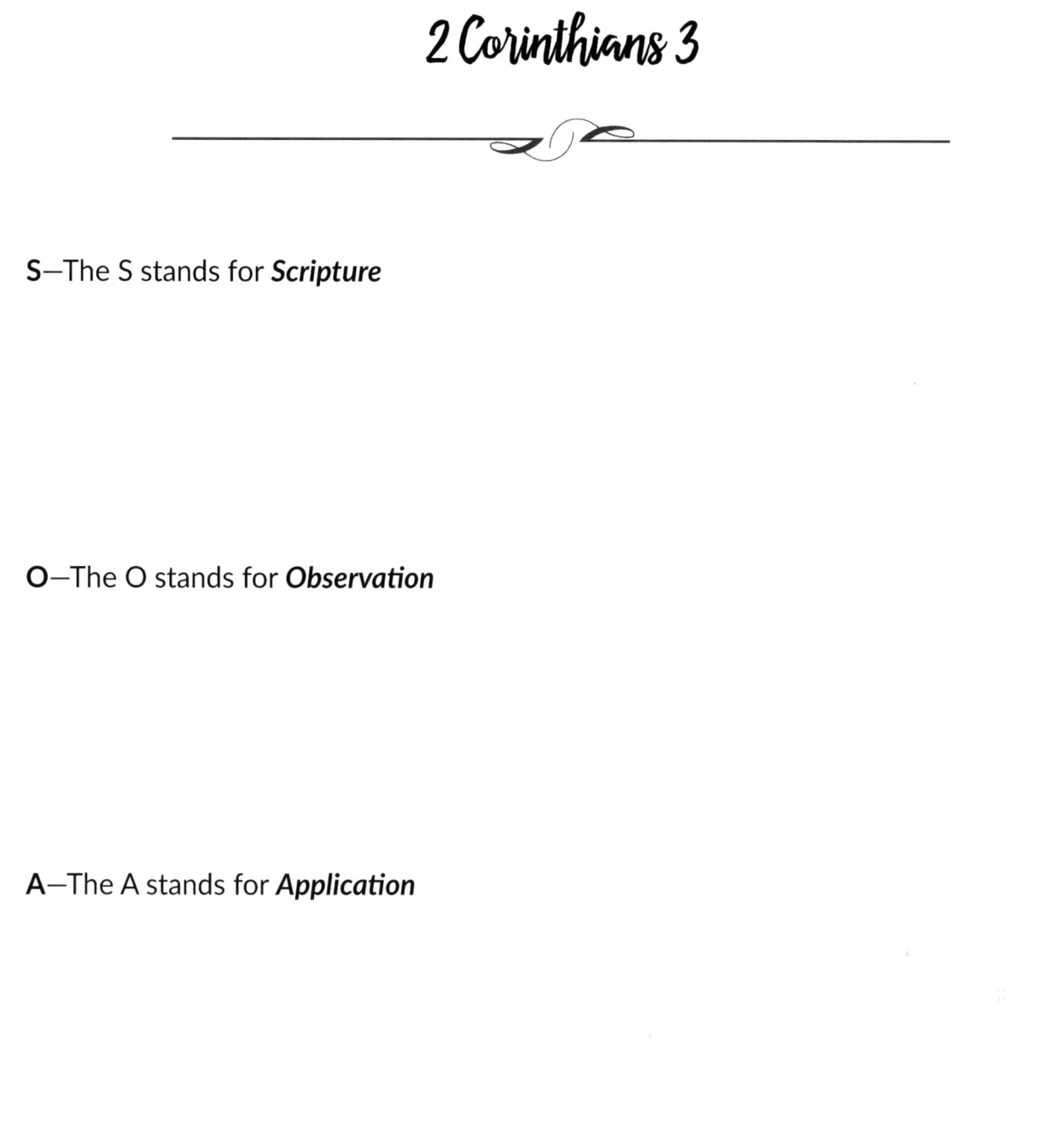

2 Corinthians 3

S—The S stands for *Scripture*

O—The O stands for *Observation*

A—The A stands for *Application*

K—The K stands for *Kneeling in Prayer*

For the things that are seen are temporary,

but the things that are unseen are eternal.

2 Corinthians 4:18

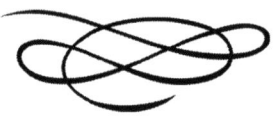

Reflection Question:

Life is short. All of the affliction we suffer here on earth is but for a moment in comparison to eternity. Until we understand the eternal weight of glory (v.17), we will not be able to see our afflictions as light. When we focus on what we see and on the temporary things of this world, life can feel unbearably hard. But when we consider the unseen world and heaven that awaits us, our troubles here on earth come into better perspective.

Sometimes our struggles can make us sad, bitter, angry, resentful and simply miserable. The more we think about our problems, the bigger they become, but the more we consider the hope that awaits us in heaven, the stronger we become. Is there something troubling you today? How does taking your focus off of that problem and focusing on the unseen world that awaits you, give you hope and strength to press on through the hard times?

2 Corinthians 4

S—The S stands for **Scripture**

O—The O stands for **Observation**

A—The A stands for **Application**

K—The K stands for **Kneeling in Prayer**

If anyone is in Christ,

he is a new creation.

The old has passed away;

behold, the new has come.

2 Corinthians 5:17

Reflection Question:

No matter who you are—if you are born again, you are more than just forgiven—you are changed! Just as God created the world, he recreates us into a new creation. Each day as we grow closer to him, he changes our hearts desires and fills us with his love, joy and peace.

Religion can change our behavior but a genuine relationship with God changes our heart. How has God changed your life? What old things have you left behind and what new things has he done in your life?

2 Corinthians 5

S—The S stands for *Scripture*

O—The O stands for *Observation*

A—The A stands for *Application*

K—The K stands for *Kneeling in Prayer*

*Go out from their midst,
and be separate from them,
says the Lord.
2 Corinthians 6:17*

Reflection Question:

Paul called on the church to separate themselves from the world. This did not mean that they were not to love and minister to unbelievers, but he wanted them to be on guard against their ungodly influence. We need to be *in* the world but not *of* the world.

Is there an ungodly bond in your life that needs to be broken? Romans 12:2 tells us, to not be conformed to the world but be transformed by the renewing of your mind. Examine your friendships, your music, movie, book and social media choices. What are some of the ungodly influences in your life that you need to separate yourself from and why?

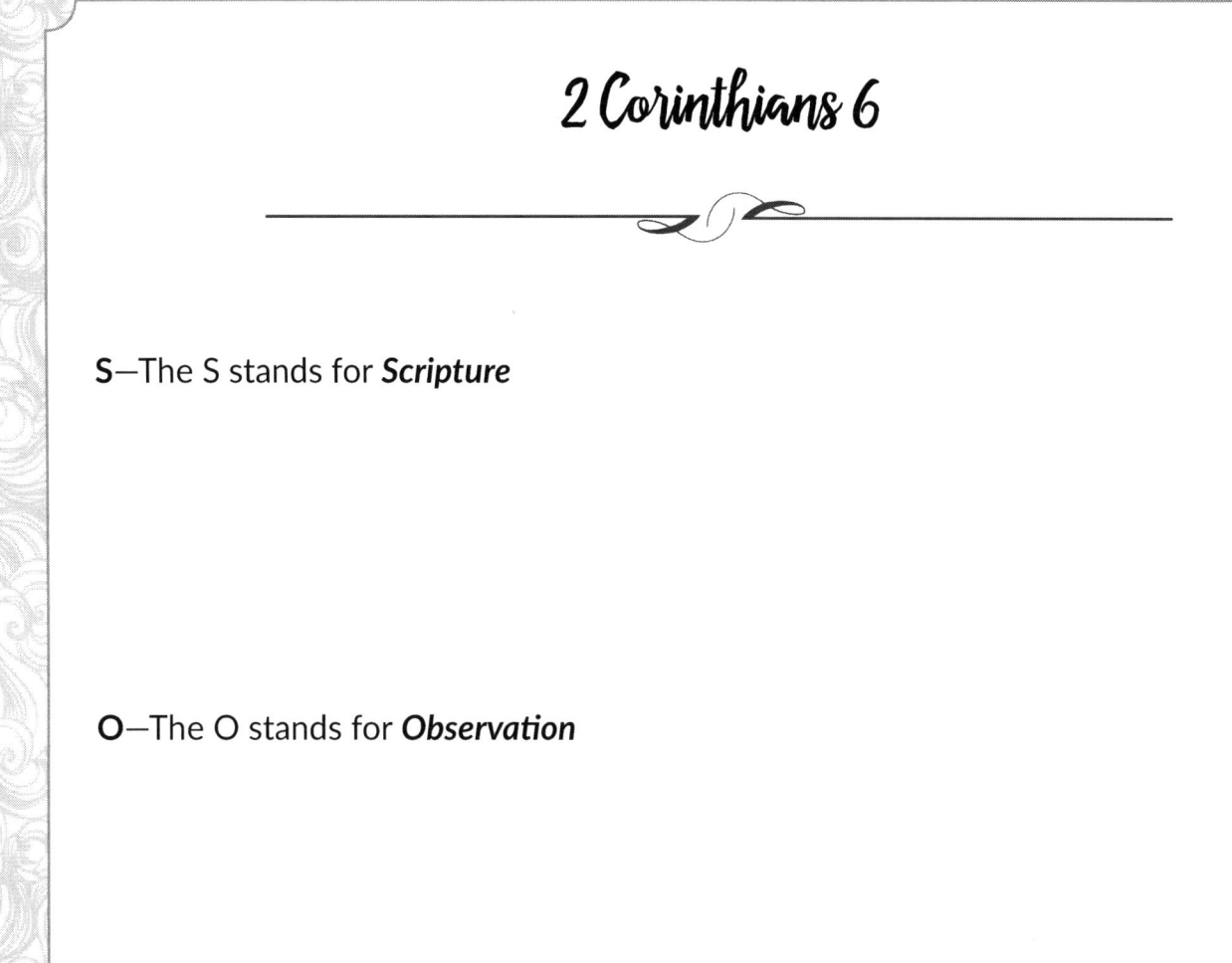

2 Corinthians 6

S—The S stands for **Scripture**

O—The O stands for **Observation**

A—The A stands for **Application**

K—The K stands for **Kneeling in Prayer**

For godly grief produces a repentance that leads to salvation without regret, whereas worldly grief produces death.

2 Corinthians 7:10

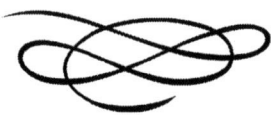

Reflection Question:

Not all sorrow over sin is godly sorrow. Some are only sorry because they got caught. But godly grief produces genuine repentance. Repentance is more evident through the actions it produces, than it is through someone's words or tears. Godly sorrow leads to sweet forgiveness, while worldly sorrow leads to regret, bad consequences and death.

Our sorrow over sin does not feel good but it is good for us because it leads to repentance. Pause and consider, when was the last time you grieved over your sin? Is there sin in your life that you need to repent of? Write a prayer of repentance below.

2 Corinthians 7

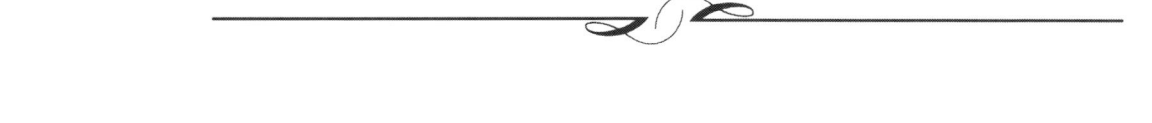

S—The S stands for *Scripture*

O—The O stands for *Observation*

A—The A stands for *Application*

K—The K stands for *Kneeling in Prayer*

But as you excel in everything

in faith, in speech, in knowledge

and in our love for you

see that you excel

in this act of grace also.

2 Corinthians 8:7

Reflection Question:

Paul wanted the Corinthian church to not just excel in faith, speech, knowledge and love but in giving as well. They may have had good intentions about giving but he wanted them to put action to their good intentions. Giving is an act of grace, that comes from God. God is the one who gives to us, so that we can give to others. Our generosity shows the work of God in our lives.

Sometimes we think of those who give financial support to ministries as people who are taking a short cut because they don't want to roll up their sleeves and do the dirty work. But that is not how God sees it. Giving shows the grace of God at work in a believer's life. Are you generous? Is there someone in need that you could help today? Is there a ministry or missionary that could use your support? Do not worry about the size of the gift. God looks at the heart. What changes do you need to make, so that you can put action to your good intentions and excel in the grace of giving?

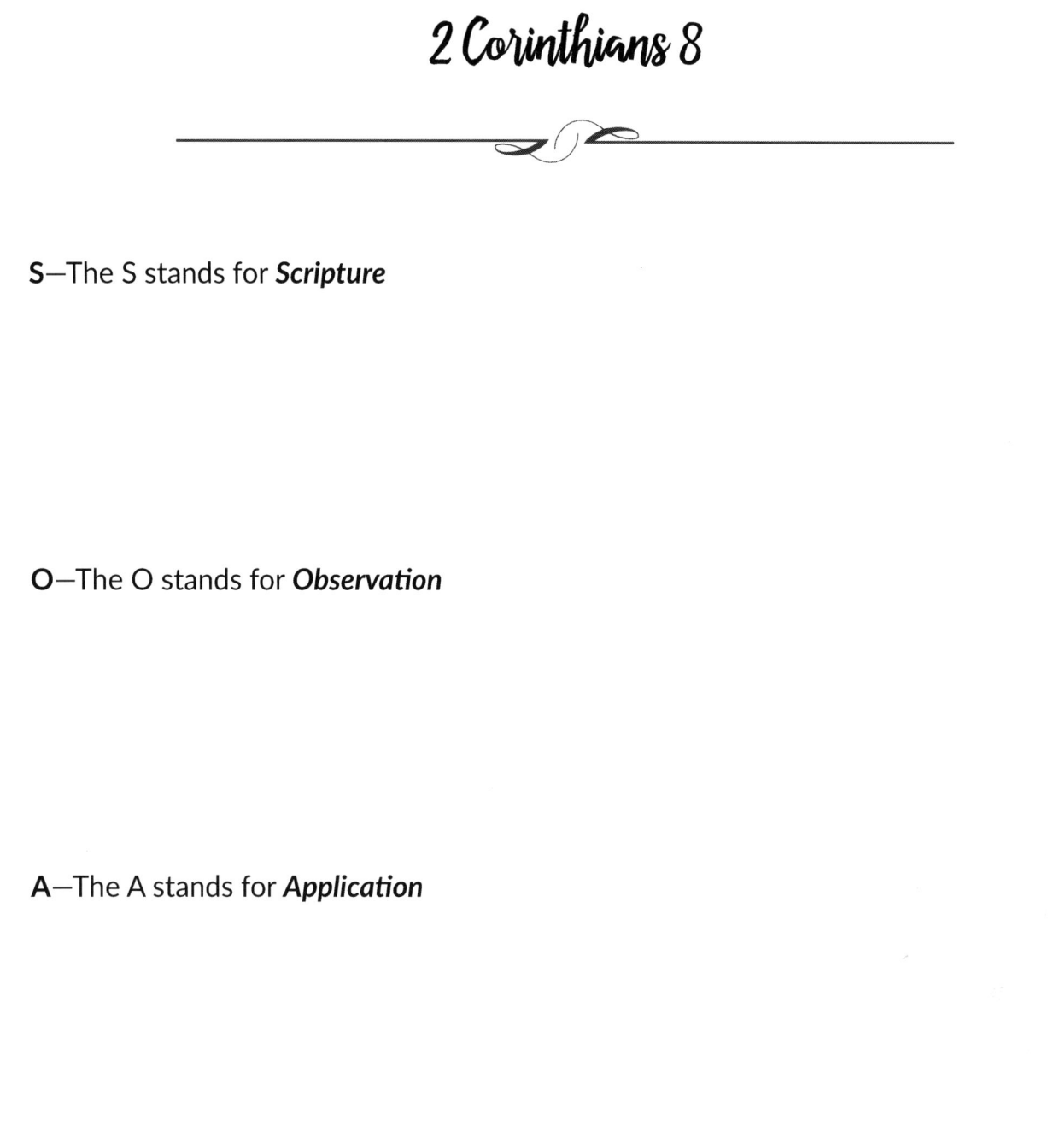

2 Corinthians 8

S—The S stands for **Scripture**

O—The O stands for **Observation**

A—The A stands for **Application**

K—The K stands for **Kneeling in Prayer**

God loves a cheerful giver.

2 Corinthians 9:7

Reflection Question:

God is a cheerful giver and he wants us to be like him and give cheerfully as well. The word cheerful here means hilarious or to be happy. God does not want us to give reluctantly or from outward pressure but instead to be happy givers.

When we give our offering, it should not feel like a tax that is forced. Instead, it should come from the overflow of a happy heart. This verse does not say that God loves when you give but that he loves a cheerful giver. God is looking at your heart. Now consider your bank account and the money that you have recently spent. Usually, how we spend our money reveals the things we love. Matthew 6:21 says, *"For where your treasure is, there your heart will be also."* When was the last time you gave to the Lord? Are you a cheerful giver?

2 Corinthians 9

S—The S stands for **Scripture**

O—The O stands for **Observation**

A—The A stands for **Application**

K—The K stands for **Kneeling in Prayer**

We destroy arguments and every lofty opinion raised against the knowledge of God, and take every thought captive to obey Christ.

2 Corinthians 10:5

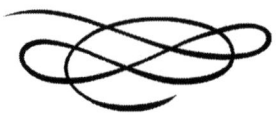

Reflection Question:

Though we live in the flesh, the war of the mind is not against flesh but against spiritual strongholds. There are those who argue and debate the truth of God, who give their lofty opinions. They come against God in our minds. Our flesh is powerless against the enemies lies, so we must take every thought captive and make it obedient to Christ.

Paul tells the Corinthian church to take "every" thought captive. Pause for a moment and reflect on your thoughts—take them captive. What ungodly opinions and arguments have you come up against lately? Have you struggled with fear, bitterness, anger, lust, greed, jealousy or other sinful thoughts? What thoughts or lies have you held on to, that need to be changed and made obedient to Christ?

2 Corinthians 10

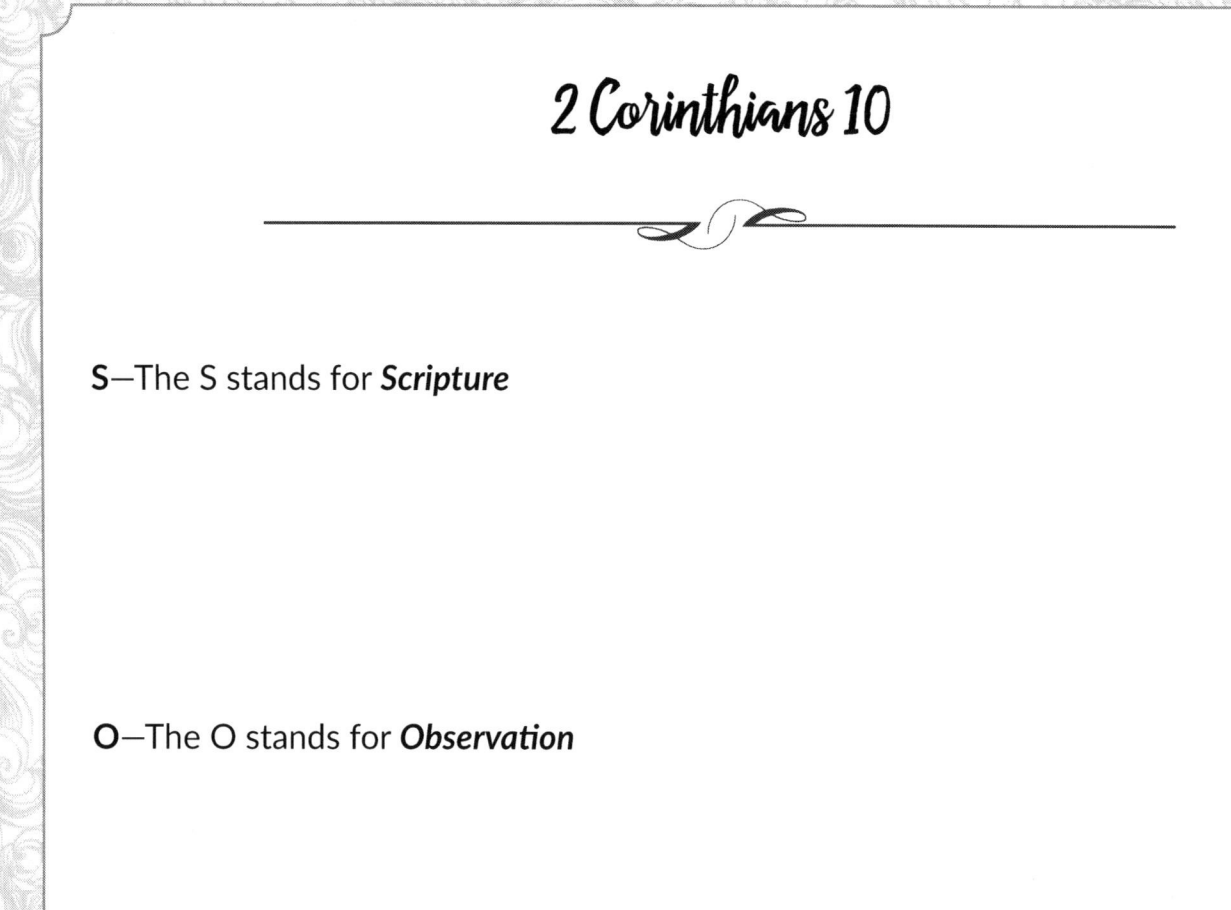

S—The S stands for **Scripture**

O—The O stands for **Observation**

A—The A stands for **Application**

K—The K stands for **Kneeling in Prayer**

Even Satan disguises himself as an angel of light.

2 Corinthians 11:14

Reflection Question:

There are some in the church who will disguise themselves as servants of God, but they are really false teachers. They may have a good appearance, but they are not of God. Instead, they are like Satan who disguises himself as an angel of light. Satan knows that believers love the light. We love goodness and truth so he doesn't present himself as dark and evil, but instead as an angel of light, so people will be drawn to his lies.

We need to beware of accepting preachers, teachers, authors and speakers just based on their outward appearance or eloquent speech. Some follow false teachers and end up deceived because they do not know God's word. We need to study the Word, so we can discern between what is true and what is false. How are you making sure you are not following a false teacher? Are you careful to examine a new preacher, teacher or author to be sure they are not a false teacher?

2 Corinthians 11

S—The S stands for *Scripture*

O—The O stands for *Observation*

A—The A stands for *Application*

K—The K stands for *Kneeling in Prayer*

"My grace is sufficient for you, for my power is made perfect in weakness."

2 Corinthians 12:9

Reflection Question:

Paul had a "thorn in the flesh" to keep him from becoming prideful and to keep him dependent on God. He said that it came from Satan, but God used it for good. The Lord was more concerned with his power being displayed through Paul's weakness, than with removing the thorn. Instead of removing it, God gave Paul more grace and more strength to keep going.

We do not know if Paul's thorn was physical, spiritual or emotional, but we do know that it hurt, and that Paul had prayed and asked the Lord to remove it. God allowed him to suffer with this thorn, so that God's power would be seen through his weakness. Do you have a thorn in your life that has humbled you and been used by God to reveal his power in your weakness? How have you experienced God's grace in the midst of your suffering?

2 Corinthians 12

S—The S stands for *Scripture*

O—The O stands for *Observation*

A—The A stands for *Application*

K—The K stands for *Kneeling in Prayer*

Finally, brothers, rejoice.
Aim for restoration, comfort one another,
agree with one another, live in peace;
and the God of love and peace will be with you.
2 Corinthians 13:11

Reflection Question:

In Paul's final words to the Corinthians, he tells them to rejoice. They should have joy because they have a relationship with the living God. He encourages them to comfort one another, agree with one another and live in peace with one another. All of these things take two to accomplish and so he challenged them to do their part. And then finally, he reminded them to always remember that the God of love and peace is with them. They are not alone.

As we close out our study in the book of 2 Corinthians, I want to encourage you to first rejoice. Choose joy and be glad that you have a relationship with God. Then consider, are you doing your part in the church to comfort other believers? How could you do this more? And are you doing your part to live in peace with other believers? It may be difficult, but it is good and pleasing to the Lord. God is with you and he loves you. Keep walking with the King?

2 Corinthians 13

S—The S stands for **Scripture**

O—The O stands for **Observation**

A—The A stands for **Application**

K—The K stands for **Kneeling in Prayer**

Made in the USA
Monee, IL
01 September 2020